DESIGNING FOR
WELLNESS

an artist's outlook on health, home and happiness

Artwork and writing by Susie Frazier

Edited by Lisa Dranuski, Elizabeth King, Carol Payto, and Chris Woodman

Photography by:

Elizabeth King (p. 2, 6, 8, 11, 15, 18, 20, 21, 24, 26, 32, 35, 36, 37, 38, 40, 41, 44, 45, 47, 48, 51, 56, 57, 58, 60, 62, 63, 67, 75)

Susie Frazier (p. 16, 17, 22, 23, 27, 28, 30, 34, 42, 46, 50, 52, 53, 61, 64, 66, 70, 72, 79)

Sarah Holden (p. 10, 12, 14, 31, 68, 71, 76)

Patrick Fraser (p. 78)

Lisa Dranuski (p. 80)

Extra love to my mom, Linda, sister, Nancy, and children, Casey, Morgan, and Brady, for your various support.

Designing For Wellness

© 2018 by Susie Frazier

All rights reserved.

Published in the United States

ISBN 978-1-54395-118-9

This book is dedicated to the artist who lives in all of us

A PATH TO WELLNESS is more than an exercise program or a nutrition plan. It's a daily practice of taking care of the mind.

When my career as a professional artist began in 1997, I had no idea I lived with anxiety and ADHD. All I knew was that my brain rarely slowed down as it tried to process thoughts, feelings, and sensory experiences simultaneously all day long. Like millions of people facing a hectic modern world, I wished for the spaces around me to be more restorative. Instead, cultural norms promoted TVs in every room, open floor plans that echoed the smallest of sounds, and cluttered collectibles that became overwhelming.

Yet when I focused on ways to connect with nature, the tension easily dissolved.

Thankfully, enough scientific research has confirmed that earth-minded materials and patterns placed in built environments bring a sense of calm to those inside them. Keeping that in mind, my hope is that you use this book as a simple reference for turning any room into your very own sanctuary. The lessons I've learned over a lifetime of coping with disquiet are all here, alongside photos of my actual process and projects.

It's my belief that the next frontier in wellness is not about the workout or the food chain. It's about designing spaces that proactively support psychological well-being.

Many benefits of the natural world can be felt by observing small ecosystems, not just wide open terrain.

become aware of the earth

When we spend any reflective time outdoors, we start to awaken to the lessons of the landscape. We see, first hand, how nature is abundantly resourceful.

The decay of one thing becomes the growth of another, presenting a fundamental truth of our world — that everything is interrelated and thrives because life is inclusive.

Although our modern settings often separate us from the outside environment, the first step toward improving our health is to realize the many ways we are emotionally and physically connected to the earth.

A spalted maple tree stump was transformed into a set of live edge tables for The Edison at Gordon Square apartment community in Cleveland.

Natural palm fronds were assembled into encaustic wax to create one of three art pieces inside The Fowler Center for Business at Case Western Reserve University.

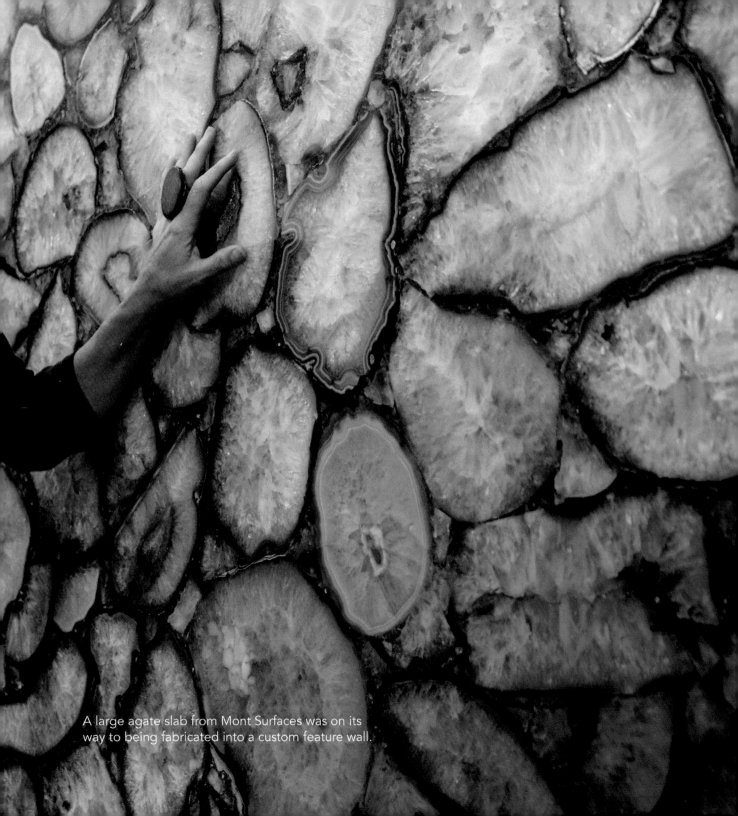

A large agate slab from Mont Surfaces was on its way to being fabricated into a custom feature wall.

focus on organic patterns

Raw elements of nature are the basis of many discoveries in math and science. Yet biotic systems have done more than influence new technology or clever consumer products. They also embody patterns that teach us how to relax.

Through small variations in repetition, organic forms demonstrate how life is slow, evolving and imperfect.

Whether it's the art on our walls or the contours in our counters, earth-inspired design subconsciously comforts us as we navigate our own experiences with change.

Salvaged wood logs were cut, sanded, and finished with a gray wash to complete this residential installation along a client's staircase wall.

Blackened stainless steel shapes were
mounted into a floating swarm installation
inside the office lobby of CM Wealth Advisors.

Organic growth patterns in tree
bark are a great resource for developing
designs with wavy contours and negative space.

Stainless steel tabletop scupltures, made for The Gordon Square Arts District, were inspired by tree bark seen in Cleveland Metroparks.

bring the outside inside ● ●

Choosing natural materials to surround us is a vital step toward healing what's within us.

Sometimes sifting through the bones of the beach is the most therapeutic act of all. This simple practice enables us, like wounded warriors, to set down the stories of our past and be selective about which ones to carry with us going forward. We learn that not every log is worth hauling home to become the centerpiece of our table.

Once we participate in the gathering and releasing of nature as part of our design process, we discover a very individualized method for supporting our psyche.

Over 34 driftwood logs were harvested from the shores of Lake Erie to create this statement piece on a client's dining room wall.

Accents made out of organic elements, like these driftwood candleholders, set a tone of casual comfort within any setting.

Found objects from nature, like this abandoned bird nest made entirely out of horse hair, can become decorative totems for helping our minds slow down.

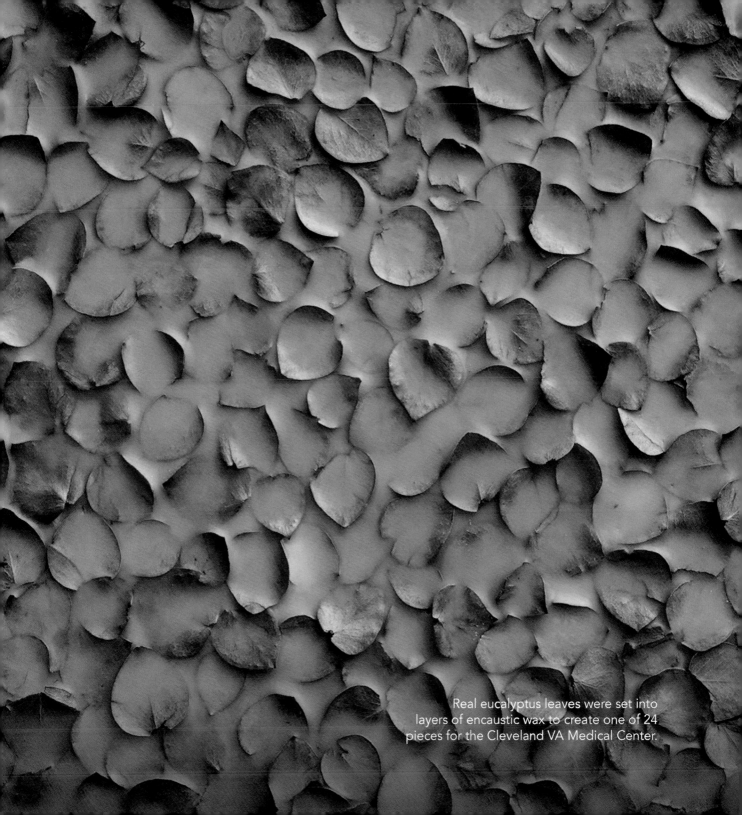

Real eucalyptus leaves were set into layers of encaustic wax to create one of 24 pieces for the Cleveland VA Medical Center.

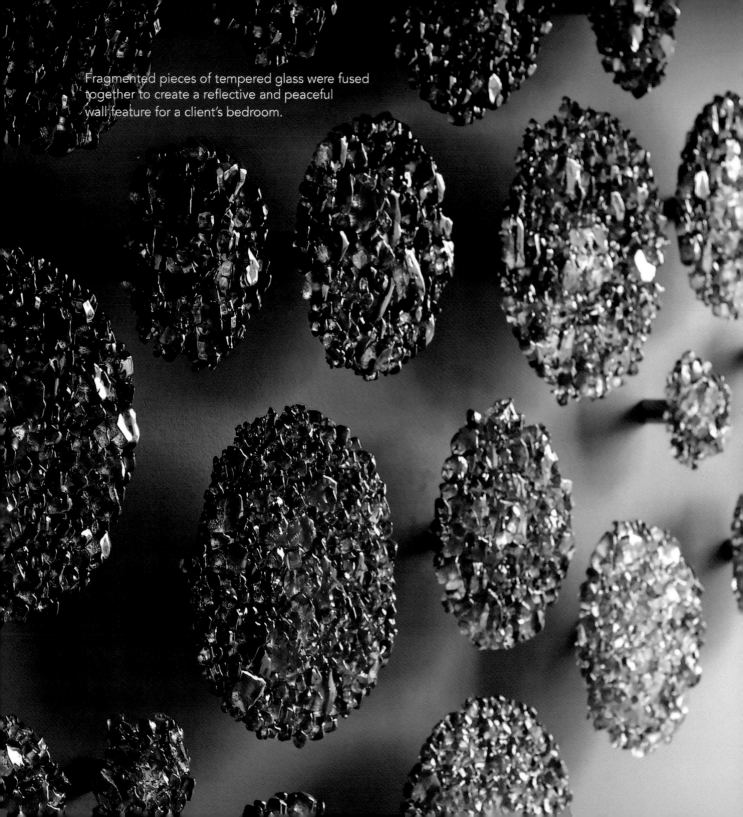

Fragmented pieces of tempered glass were fused together to create a reflective and peaceful wall feature for a client's bedroom.

make the broken beautiful

One of the most empowering skills we can acquire is the act of transforming loose fragments into something new.

Makers do this by forming raw materials into art. Writers do it by arranging words to build a story. And musicians do it by combining notes to compose a song. When we reframe the pieces of our lives into fresh and appealing outcomes, we learn to think like a designer.

Well-planned spaces should always feature elements that remind us how to reclaim, renew, and repeat.

When we recognize the beauty in nature's breakdown,
we learn to appreciate the beauty in ourselves.

Dried grass stalks and encaustic wax were formed into Zen-like artwork for Southwest General Hospital.

Salvaged blueprints were cut, bent and hardened around wire to create a free-form wall installation inside a model suite at the Edge 1909 apartment community in Pittsburgh.

embrace the imperfections ●

Living by impossible ideals is a habit that keeps us from wellness. Spotless spaces and impeccable furniture make anyone feel like they can't be themselves, which leads to an ongoing state of dis-ease.

A need for perfection creates unnecessary tension in our bodies, our relationships, and even our homes through the decorative decisions we make.

If we truly care about nurturing health over the long haul, our settings need to tastefully feature the flaws rather than eliminate them.

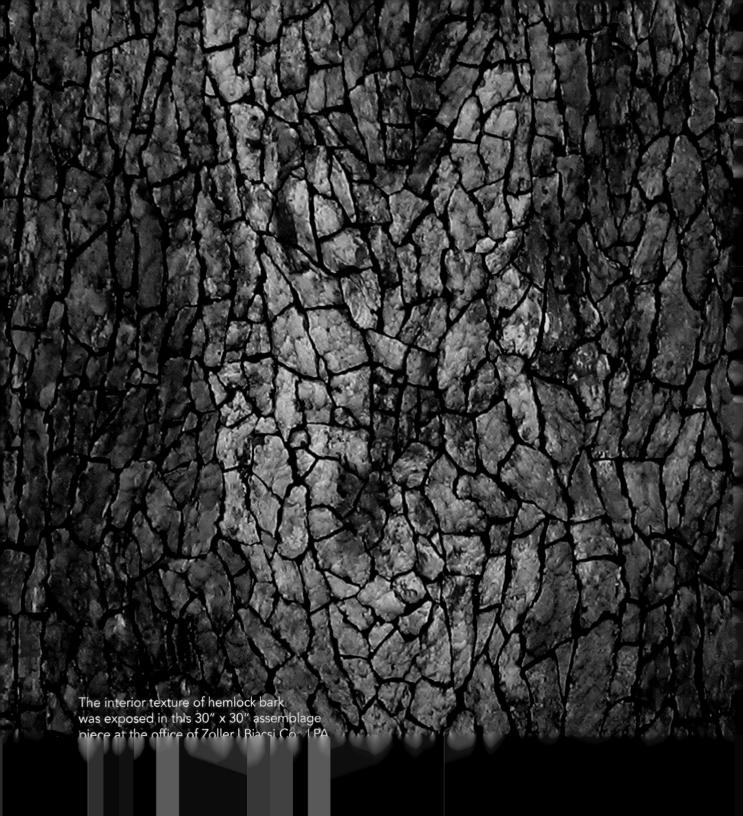

The interior texture of hemlock bark was exposed in this 30" x 30" assemblage piece at the office of Zoller | Biacsi Co., | PA.

Reclaimed wood beams from Saint Catherine Church in Cleveland were converted into a rustic modern table for Kimpton Rowan Palm Springs Hotel.

feed your soul with color

So much of our modern life is spent in man-made settings without access to nature, which puts our mood at risk and blocks the positive effects earth tones can have on our spirit.

As an alternative, taking walks outside to see the deep shades of a forest after a rain or the bold pigments of a prairie at dawn can awaken us to the calming affects of color.

When we allow outdoor settings to inspire us at the most basic levels, we can discover which hues are most ideally suited to our homes.

Dried eucalyptus fused into encaustic wax adds peaceful tones any room.

Time spent outdoors searching for
fallen earth fragments can inspire
many decorative ideas at home.

Fresh cut greens inside steel and glass wall vases adds vitality to a workspace inside the headquarters of Organic Spa Magazine.

Grass stalks from a backyard landscape were embedded into layers of encaustic wax to complement the color scheme of a client's farmhouse.

River rocks on an open table bring comfort to restless minds by offering a tactile object for the hands to play with.

integrate tactile elements ●

When we immerse ourselves in settings in which everything is smooth to the touch, we inhibit our ability to perceive the world around us.

That's why texture is so important in our built environments.

Items that are accessible to handle activate our senses and provide an instrument for building awareness. The more conscious we are in our physical experiences, the more responsive we are in our emotional ones.

The way our spaces make us feel should always be paramount to the way our spaces look.

A custom wooden headboard features engraved
contours to provide both a tactile and visual experience.

Tables with built in trays for touching loose beans, shells, rice or rocks become a decorative tool for reducing stress.

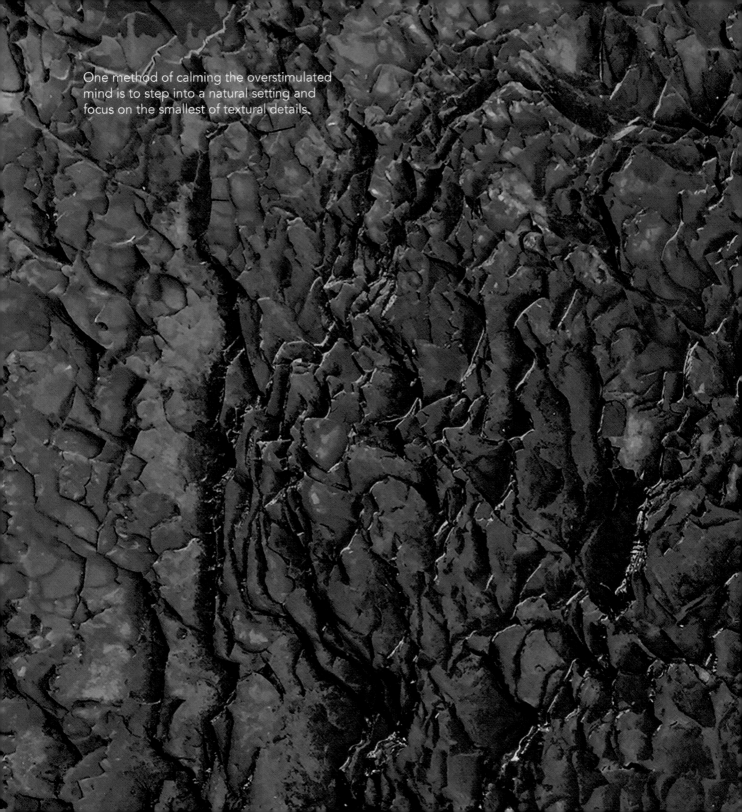

One method of calming the overstimulated mind is to step into a natural setting and focus on the smallest of textural details.

disconnect from the noise ●

Every day we're subjected to an onslaught of sounds, whether it's scanners at retail stores or commercials at the gas pump. It seems like everywhere we turn, we're exposed to anything but silence.

Consider this the next time you're at a doctor's office or a restaurant listening to blaring music, buzzing video games, and rowdy TV shows all at once. Sometimes we need brain rest from unsolicited noise, especially when it exists in our own homes.

If we want to cultivate more composure within us, we need to turn off the racket around us.

Organic patterns seen in these steel sculptures for
The Society for Marketing Professional Services
offer a visual distraction for tuning out noise.

Relaxing in outdoor spaces, away from technology, provides many restorative benefits to our brain.

A sense of stillness can be created by designing with subdued colors and textures, like those found within this 12" coco twig piece for The Cleveland VA Medical Center.

A floating wood installation
was made to generate a feeling
of calm inside the lobby of University
Hospitals North Ridgeville Health Center.

choose art that holds meaning

The artifacts we hang in a place say a lot about the respect we have for those who inhabit it.

When we select high-quality work that triggers a positive feeling or features an enriching story, we're providing opportunities for people to have a fulfilling experience associated with the setting.

The visuals we position around us are capable of curating any state of mind imaginable. All the more reason why the art of a space should never be an afterthought.

A grass assemblage piece, made for Nordson Corporation, used materials found near their Ohio headquarters, tying the art to a specific place.

Hand drawn schematics from
the 1960s were cut and collaged onto
reclaimed wood, offering an interesting backstory.

Real gravel used in Fairmount Santrol's high
performance, sand-based products were designed
into an art series given to their retiring chief executive officer.

Immersing ourselves in outdoor landscapes can provide new perspectives on the kind of visuals we'd like to see throughout our interiors.

To create a haven where you can ground your soul,
be sure to fill it with your favorite things.

create a space for solitude

Most people today enjoy very little quiet time. It's here, without interruptions, where we can generate our best ideas, concentrate on a single task, and give our imagination room to play.

When we carve out simple, silent spaces to disengage from the frenzy, we are reconnecting to a slower, more natural flow of life where it's finally possible to daydream.

Whether it's a bedroom, a back office, or a private porch, dedicated places of rest are vital to nourishing emotional wellness.

A television-free bedroom, with a custom headboard cut out of wood, provides a sanctuary for sleep.

A simple oasis can be made by bringing your indoor seating to the outdoors.

Organic wood magnets on a blackened steel panel provide a functional and hands-on feature inside an executive's office at Nordson Corporation.

● offer something interactive ● ●

If nature teaches us anything, it's that living things flourish through change.

Expose a plant to an environment filled with obstacles, and you'll see it adjust to the new conditions. Like vines twisting through trees to reach sunlight, adaptations are more than instincts to survive. They're cultivated traits for surviving well.

Intuitively, humans are the same way.

Provide people with architecture that's designed to move or surroundings that are easily switched, and we'll witness thriving creatures inspired by opportunities to grow.

Mind-calming desktop sculptures, with spinning steel components, were given to Crain's Cleveland 40 Under 40 award recipients as a way to unwind at work.

Bowls of sand provide an soothing opportunity
to engage the mind with ever-changing patterns.

Collecting dried materials from nature reduces stress and provides organic accents for your home or office.

Creating artwork out of fallen earth fragments is a form
of biophilia that adds tranquility to any space.

Right-sized nesting tables and softer elements
can create a comfortable corner in any room.

develop intimate nooks

There's a reason why babies settle down in a swaddled blanket and why animals assemble in nests. They feel safe and comfortable when they're surrounded on all sides.

The same is true for most of us. Cozy spaces that offer warmth and an ambient glow naturally feel better than vaulted rooms with too many lights.

Whether it's an alcove to read, a chamber for sleep, or a corner to be creative, a snug hideaway can provide a reprieve from tension and a boost to productivity.

Small textural art, like this milkweed and encaustic wax piece made for Southwest General Hospital, creates a mini moment to personally connect with the natural world.

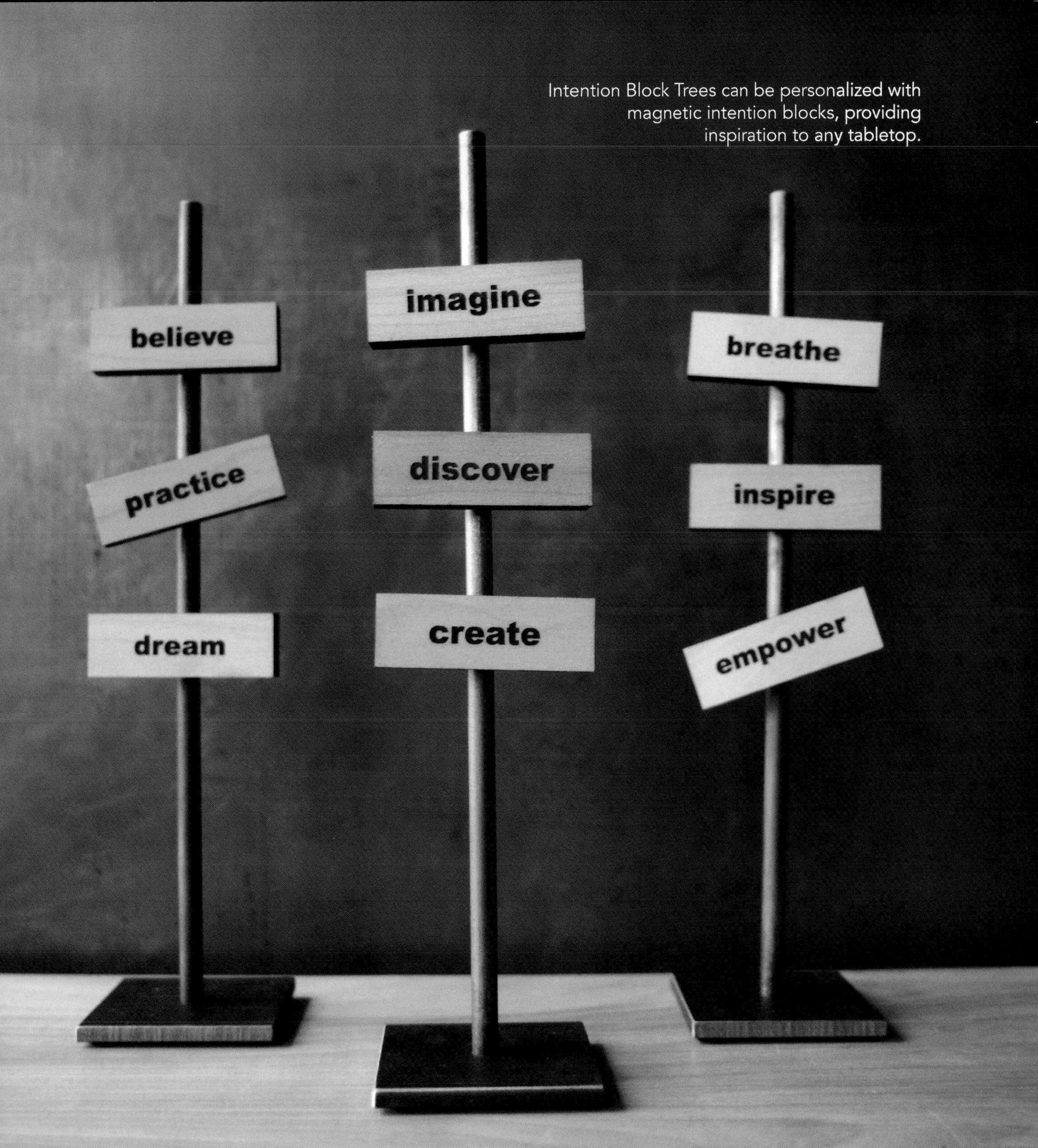

Intention Block Trees can be personalized with magnetic intention blocks, providing inspiration to any tabletop.

believe

imagine

breathe

practice

discover

inspire

dream

create

empower

Repeating crescent patterns ripple along
a wall at BakerHostetler law firm in Cleveland.

curate positivity ●

Everything in our world embodies energy. Wind, water, rocks, and
creatures all have degrees of receiving and radiating. Even the
accents placed in our homes carry a vibration that can affect
anyone who enters.

Once we awaken to the impact our collectibles have on us, we can
learn to harness the power of our possessions to enhance our
well-being.

Much like the people we meet along our way, if a decorative
element doesn't generate a positive feeling, it doesn't belong in
our lives.

Found driftwood is a humble reminder to connect with what's authentic in ourselves.

A metal cutout for Dawn Cook Design adds rhythm and a sense of wonder to a client's wall.

Assembling like-minded elements together is a simple
way to keep collections neat, like this original art made out
of several hundred driftwood pieces found along Lake Erie.

establish a sense of order

Creating calm in the mind begins with being organized in our space.

All too often, our places of rest are filled with chaotic visuals that do little to help us decompress. Cluttered counters and crowded accessories can accumulate until we're unable to shake the feeling of being buried. That's when it's time to clear out the excess.

If we want to feel more serenity, we need to advocate for more simplicity.

Variations in repeating patterns, as seen in this 46' long
wood installation for Cuyahoga Community College, remind
us that fluid form provides an easfulness that straight lines cannot.

Stacks of salvaged wood are an exciting resource for adding an heirloom quality to home improvements or custom furniture.

don't hesitate to renovate

Even the best revamps involve some kind of turmoil.

Like it or not, construction by way of destruction is part of the natural order. It's how our planet makes room for new life. It's how communities become reinvented, and it's how our very own body heals itself.

Although we often find ourselves avoiding any discomfort that causes upheaval to our personal environments, there are times when pulling down the paneling and knocking out a wall is exactly what it takes to bring the light back into our lives.

Dried grapevine bark was collected and assembled, strand by strand, into one of two dozen artworks for the Cleveland VA Medical Center.

put it all into practice

Designing for wellness takes into account individuals with sensitive minds. As bellwethers for the emotional state of society, we feel the strain of a lifestyle that's unsustainable. Because of that, we are in a unique position to help steer our culture back to a healthier way to live. The journey starts with the choices we make for our own personal spaces.

Become Aware of The Earth, explore nearby landscapes

Focus On Organic Patterns, integrate nature's details

Bring The Outside Inside, decorate with found objects

Make The Broken Beautiful, piece together something new

Embrace The Imperfections, highlight what has character

Feed Your Soul With Color, broaden the spectrum

Integrate Tactile Elements, add texture to every room

Disconnect From The Noise, reject the barrage of sounds

Choose Art That Holds Meaning, make your setting matter

Create A Space For Solitude, prioritize places to daydream

Offer Something Interactive, add features that favor growth

Develop Intimate Nooks, create cozy spaces that feel safe

Curate Positivity, highlight items that give off good energy

Establish A Sense of Order, simplify various collections

Don't Hesitate To Renovate, accept the chaos in creativity

See more design tips when you stay connected:

Web Site: susiefrazier.com
Instagram: @susiefrazier
Facebook: @susie.frazier.cleveland
Pinterest: @susiefraziercle
YouTube: Susie Frazier